a mouthful of sky

poems
by
anu mahadev

Get Fresh Publishing, A Non-Profit Corp.
PO Box 901,
Union, NJ 07083

www.gfbpublishing.org

cover art:
Maria Valdivia

typesetting/design:
culture glut llc
cultureglut.com

This book was typeset in Bembo.

To women who are the swaying branches in a storm
— you *are* the storm.

"We are amazed how hurt we are.
We would give anything for what we have."

—Tony Hoagland

"our hands are light blue and gentle
our eyes are full of terrible confessions"

—Anne Sexton

table of contents

eight days till the new moon

1. she bites into a cheeseburger without realizing
   there's beef in it.
   will it be the cane or the boot, this time, she palpitates?

2. she agrees to anything he says. she'll change for him.
   gets her atoms ready in the reactor.

3. "so what is the big deal if you forget to shave
   your legs? surely
   the stubble won't hurt as much in bed?"
   she can't tell her friend
   everything is always a big deal.

4. her eyebrows are dense forests, mixed with blood.
   he wants her
   to wax them. they hide her acne. which he hates too.

5. who invented this torture device, the cellphone?
   the greyhound
   takes four hours — houston to austin. he calls her an
   asshole for four hours.
   she cannot hang up. the bus has to keep moving.

6. car dealerships are stressful for her. car lingo, sales
   jargon, he helps her negotiate. hands the keys. in the
   car — he rams her head against the steering wheel, till
   a satisfied grunt escapes his lips. and then he looks
   for the gps.

7. winter months. she hovers near the fridge.
   soup or candy bar?
   a post-it is stuck to the handle. his neat writing
   — her weight on it. she steps back, stumbles against
   the weighing scale by mistake. flees the kitchen.

8. he wants to get married. with a noose instead
   of a mangalsutra. she stays up,
   writing pros and cons, like balancing
   an accounts ledger.

lip gloss

two cylindrical tubes
stand next to each other
austere, proud

encase the thick languid
liquid in chambers of
plastic and fine steel.

colors clash and complete
the spectrum —
raspberry, boysenberry

i open one, cloying
sweet smell of ripe fruit arrests
me. promise of a kiss,

glittering stars in my mouth
linger as i paint the satin,
i can taste youth

squeezed from a tube, rush
of beauty, aromatic midnight.
i prop it up, admire its reflection

shimmering with the sun like
a pylon of light, drawing me back
into its waxy venus fly trap

every time. my age, my half-life
forgotten, as long as it rests

loftily on my lips, a perfect pout
staining the chipped teacup.

rain

1.

this season reminds me of strawberries
and cream, sucked into my mouth.

cream that coats my breasts, a tulle fog.
dark skin, simmering in salty sweat.

you part my legs, take in the absence of those
black clouds of hair. you find me nude, wanting.

2.

mouth of the sun, yours, hot, melting. fusing
with my legs. city of dreams. slender fingers,

granite hands, divide me, firm, gentle,
purposeful. sultry summer, this union

wrung away in monsoon's slush, roads
of potholes, roads to my body, my navel.

3.

senseless loose lush burning light,
light of your caramel eyes

blinding, searing my throat, your name,
your throbbing pounding name,

beating on my lips, the name of hunger

kairos

i am beyond all rules, decorum, faux images, ropes

that bind. nothing to me that the days are brumous,

sunless, & grey winters loom ahead. i stand at the shores

of the atlantic, a mistpouffer's mysterious sound floats to me,

dense fog. this is that perfect, delicate, moment—that kairos.

when i ask for you & the waves refuse, & some god laughs

in my face. a brief drizzle of sirimiri splashes

my eyes, that see the brontide approach, you in tow.

storm

there are lists to explain, you and me in bed, naked,
without sound, electric as lightning over the sierras.

that which exists, in us, is skin to soul,
salt to brow, clear to the eye,
like voltage, red-blue fire, sheer raw sun,
rising over rim-rock.

how easily we've forgotten that song,
that ravaging cyclone, its
aftermath, lush static of grass, midnight streets,
alive with your lens.

you and i are now beautiful habits, as thunder rises
above the ridges,
crests and troughs, rumbles upstream and down
in this dry valley.

no rain is lost.

love in galvanized sheets of white heat, takes over,
while mercury
shoots skyward, pulsates to the beat of a cardiogram.

the night is some grim experiment of thunder
herniating over aurorae,
charged particles climbing over horizons, captured
in helical shapes of galaxies.

we thrash about, fall like snow in a globe,
colors in a fabergé paperweight, replete,
messy to a crimson crescendo.

contained in each other,
our soft insides invade our concavity,
with the passion of a southwest tempest,
now moving away.

leaving

but when is ever a leaving
so swift

even as the waves
crash upon the rocks, they depart
from the reluctant sand tarmac, ever so slowly — like

window-wash liquid drips on a heart-pane,
only to be wiped out in slow-measured strokes — like

red wine settles into the glass, its sediments floating

carelessly
along the curves, unhurried,
downwards the arc of the meniscus,

the classy way you saunter, not looking back,
the thrill of the chase
over, with me in your pocket — like

dozens of others, spiral seashells abandoned,
tossed into the waters,
smelling of stale breadcrumbs and sunburnt pennies,
a faint scent of rot, from the fading glory of youth.

photographer

i leave it to you, jet setter,
when to fade out, when to focus.

snapshots of time, captured neatly in that white nikon,
don't tell the stories they should.

anchors are boring, perhaps.

it gets old, doesn't it? constant travel to escape life?
holding onto the mirage of a free bird?

the beauty lies in me, not in what you show me.

i thought you were interesting,
until i found out that's just a synonym for insecurity,

what you hide — prints in a dark room,
guard what's not really there.

elenore

this day
when
ultraviolet spells skim in overcast skies
mirrors melt into a million stars
lost wayfarers drift in cosmic winds —

this day,
monday is just a day
you are just a rambling flaw
and elenore is just a song. just a song.

brazilian

how apt, the caterpillar hair of my pubis,
transformed to the denuded airline strip,
hot dripping wax, tender skin, raging red bumps.

all for the promise of you.

you said polygamy wasn't a sin,
i could share. i don't like to share. will this
bring you to my bedroom instead of hers?

butterfly legs — the wax stylist says in stiff tones — i slide
my cream ecru linen skirt high up my waist,
slip out of my black panties,
all within reach, air tinted with faint disapproval.

i bring the house down with my screams.

what happens in a soundproof room
stays there, with a 20% tip. i wince, waddle
like a penguin, and then i feel it. the cliché.

the power of my hairless beauty.

i don't follow a precedent, or any rules,
shameless, proud.

calm before the ravishment.

how to break a married woman

1. call her sexy, baby. even if she doesn't like it.
elevate her to the skies, to the rims of her beautiful eyes.

2. send her lusty emoticons as she struggles with the praise.
prop her on a pedestal. she wants to pout and pose.
like a vogue model.

3. she is not dark, she is dusky. she is not silly,
she is sweet 16. she is not a homemaker,
she is a wild fantasy. say you'll spank her butt.

4. keep her up past 3am. let the adrenaline rush
leach her insides. let her lose weight rapidly.

5. ignore her completely next day. don't reply.
bad boy. avoid her constant chatter, desperate alphabet.

6. don't ever talk about your wife, kids, family.
make her talk, talk a lot. talk a lot about you, baby.

7. catch her when she's alone, vulnerable.
when her husband is out of town.
when you are out of town, in a hotel.
call her from the airport.
remind her of the time you both
were on a flight together and never spoke.

8. have her talk dirty to you. ask her to send a glass
of wine with lipstick marks on it.
or come to you in a lacy thong. nothing else.

9. fuck her, hard, slowly. make her come.
have her scream your name.
naked on the bed. writhing. blow her brains out.

10. next day: leave her to sort through her feelings herself,
pummel through the day, barrel through her thoughts.
let her regret.

11. no more sexual innuendo.
let her deal with the wakened beast.
keep asking her for stripped-down photos.

12. insult her. insult her marriage.

13. cut off all contact, snip through her apologies.
make her feel like
she's doing or saying something wrong all the time.

14. alone, she'll pick up the pieces of her efforts,
her marriage, her sex.

folly

disposable heart, pickled in a jar.
i've learned to bottle it in formalin,

like other women before me,
capillaries strung out in a tangled heap.

do i need an abacus to count the slices
of time frittered away in spaces

where desperation only ricochets
into an echo? there's something to be said

about the ones like me, who accept such scraps.
and about the ones whose narcissism precedes them.

flavors of the month can't be preserved
past the expiry dates. the contents sour into acids,

leaching empty chests. sadly, when it's all over,
you still call the shots.

i'm here when you need me, here when you don't.

housewife

soap suds, silver strands of hair.
hands that move quickly, stir pots,

make lives happen. unmade beds
wait. it's been long since she said

something important. a catalog
of stains speak of the productive

days lived (not hers) outside scrubbed
walls. her life is that seemingly

endless dry cycle after the wash,
each minute counts. what comes out

are things, more things, that wait
to be used by others, not middlemen.

her dreams, shrouded in caked salt
lie ashore, she blows the wind for

others' sailboats. sometimes
she hears shadows speak in

stolen moments, when her voice
cuts sharper than light, sound

barriers broken. a central cog, she spins
invisible. life happens in grocery lines.

fortunes sometimes live in coupons.

in the bedroom

damask curtains. egyptian cotton sheets.
dust ruffle. immaculately folded.

she sits on a corner of the bed, careful
not to disturb the precision.

one micro-movement and she's
smoke. the migraine sears through her

battered nerves. she has cast herself into
a hologram. with names a la avatar.

strongest in daytime. he leaves her every time.
only the method varies.

she screams at the phantom limb
pain from her non-existent heart.

it's been carved out with a butcher's knife.
she is on fire. this is the agony she must suffer

to be a poet. she sits motionless at 7am, 2pm,
9pm, doesn't matter — on the same turned-out

corner of the same bedspread. holding her knees
together. keeping herself from spilling out.

she stares at the bottle of sleeping pills. her eyes
dart to the telephone. still in pajamas, she waits.

august

caffeinated sun. my unforgiving sweat.
i want to forget a birthday

but then it looms so large i start the countdown
a month before.

hourglass paralyzed with fear, not sure how to react

my fingers chafe through the past, fiddle with the future.

people murmur around me — she's the broken one —
shade their eyes in horror.

i radiate the burnt pain of a glass blower's kiln.

what good are promises if they're not meant for you

so, i knit. i knit a lot these days. the soft alpaca wool cuts
through my guilty palms.

the pattern goes like this.
k1 - knit a word of apology,
p2- purl a twist of self-worth until the row ends. repeat.
bind off. become whole again.

it almost works.

except — thoughts don't hide behind delicate painted
screens. they confront you — until you stumble on rocks
and you can't dislodge yourself.

what about us — who catch the wounded as they free fall
what about the ones who glue their insecurities while
agreeing to crumble into vacuum

i sail through sea waves in my flimsy schooner.
sometimes in a gale, sometimes in the doldrums.

all my clouds live in the same bipolar sky.

horoscope : leo/virgo

this is no saga. a mere spot in time's
magic scarf. i spool it out of my hat.

any number of words, colors unfurl.
handshake, a hug, a peck on my cheek.

baggage claim, you wait at the gate.
suit, tie, long coat. straight from work.

power lines around your eyes, that quizzical
smile. you know i like flowers. you still

won't bother to bring some. that arrogance!
it works. i tremble, knees quake, feet wobble.

i play it cool. somewhere the tension erupts.
a bar in san francisco, legs careful not to touch.

shots of patron. half moon bay, moonlit skies,
heartbeat throbs of waves. glasses of malbec,

night wind ruffles your hair, churns mine.
a penthouse, floor to ceiling windows, us,

mere silhouettes in the dark, ambient light.
snifters of cognac. brown eyes. besotted fingers

twist, the soft centers of our bodies crumble,
cotton sheets knotted. no promises. no lines

to cross, no moral compass. only unfinished
business. a $100 superbowl bet, spent on drinks.

the lingering possibilities thereafter. your signature
on the check, ravenous, wild. your unibrow, the way

the pen rests in your left hand. i wish i were the pen.
one night of brahma lasts more than a billion years.

this hotel room is my altar. all else is happenstance.

schism

a suitcase of stuffed printed clothes i unpack,
let the dryer-sheet scented fabric mingle

with the burnt woodsmoke smell next door.
it lingers — uneasy in the air, wafting to my face.

these clothes once belonged to the loom,
mystic, ancient; now, simply clinical, starched

from the dry-cleaners. tomorrow they will hang,
soaked under the tropical kerala sun, asking

for forgiveness from the land of their birth. does
moisture belong to a cloud? a cloud to a country?

will the sweaty kurta i wore in new york wash
in the slicing rain, in the clear ground water,

piped through the ubiquitous containers,
finally, be clean of my sins? i wring out dry

the limp dupatta, which doesn't belong anywhere
except to a closet, a moving body, a fragment of time.

i bring my scars here to be fixed, take the soap suds
from my mom's bucket, fail to glimpse those scars

she wears, with no pride or choice at all. i adorn
these morphed nuclei of threads, follow her to all

the forgotten paths of my childhood, with no hope
to reclaim the lost me. impervious, i sit, the wet clothes

cling to my body, beg me for mercy, beg to belong.

thinking of my husband during the malabar monsoon

at least once an hour

                    he walks into my mind

like the seasonal reverse wind

                    in this towel-soaked air.

rain tumbles off the bright

                    orange sloping terra cotta

tiles on my roof.

                    impervious ceramic, porous clay,

its slant drips the water

                    from the cumulonimbus cloud.

water pours from the vapors

                    of the arabian sea, bay of bengal,

the indian ocean.

                    malabar coastal shores, coconut palms,

ransack my limpid senses

                    like coffee bean crates in these three months.

arabica seeds lose their acidity,

                    i brew the coffee, pungent spice, nuts—

in its musty, chocolate aroma

                    he and i linger, touch, fall with the storm.

northeast well, kerala

in a placid enclave, dulcet whispers,

a green patina of moss, lichen,

chipped walls, a faux mask

peels with bygone days. draped in fine

lace cobwebs, occasionally targeted

by a maverick coconut or papaya.

a canopy of overhanging banana

leaves and branches of drumstick

trees cast their shadows on bushes

of sugandhi, kanakambaram flowers.

echo of the clink of copper pots, glass

bangles and measured laughter,

now — minerals float to the top

of the inert surface. like my heart,

once a fountainhead of unending

water tables, now a caked veneer

sits tranquil, oblivious to the hubbub

surrounding its stone-lipped column.

detox spiral without my lover

it has been 24 hours without my phone.
everyone thinks it is working. that you are gone.

this forced detox. you are invading my veins.
you define narcissism, magnetism, charm.

there are no formalities. for years i kept
chasing your shadows in sidewalks.

now you want to come inside me.
no birth-control. we will deal with whatever

consequences. like, a baby. with your caramelized
eyes. stop. i cannot listen to this spiel any more.

but i do listen to all the ghazals you sent.
did you really mean them? my blood rushes

to the surface. you say they are not just words.
they are how we live this one life. one love.

one god. i am blessed. i am cursed.
we will happen someday. that is certain.

you're making a kentucky mule, which i had to
google. you're reading. sexy. we are horny all the time.

you are kissing me with your lips, your tongue.
you're hungry. i can't keep up with your mercurial moods.

i am to be released from my curfew. my body
is a prison. i've heard that love sets you free?

you're telling me things. good morning gorgeous.
the code is love. the code is legs. spread the code.

in a name

devour my bare body each night,
drink from my navel, watch me surrender

to your errant tongue. your mouth anoints
me with moonrise, i'm awash in your

brown eyes. midnight swirls a torment
of black silk, you single me

out through the eyelets of my meshed
burqa, signal me with your smile.

my lips taste cloth, my eyelashes brush
against lace. i once wore jasmine in my hair,

a bindi on my forehead. cast off, to your
tethered smiles, hidden veils, the raiment

of a thousand storms, i follow you, a trailing
creeper, share you with others,

take what i get of you, to get this moniker,
in an incense-filled room of our house,

in my old city, across the five bridges.
where the call of the muezzin drowns out

all temple bells' chimes, you lavish me with
ghazals, i learn to write from right to left.

ultramarine

monday morning warrior, briefcase, pressed
pinstripe suit and tie, the promise of a nubile body
next to you.

i'm that person, and i may not be whole —
just enough to fill you.

you only see my nakedness as perfection,
not the broken bits inside,
i so desperately fix with makeshift glue,
each time i sink into your
cerulean depths.

perhaps i'd rather be alone today,
holed up in my world, calculating
my density = mass of reality/volume of dreams,
gauging the guarded smile beyond those arctic eyes.

tomorrow is too far away, i'm gambling it all
away for the promise
that some intelligent words might actually escape
my filthy mouth.

you don't want to hear them, as long as they do your job,
sing your praises.

this ephemeral firefly can't make it too far away, i think
and i've never seen
such a blue night sky, before the rains
come crashing, drowning me,
sumac in a shaker jar.

a mouthful of sky

i.

there are days
                    i'm passing myself off as anita in a wig
of insults & nonstop wild sex
                       to the curious friendly passenger
in other words
                    easy target — no ring on finger —
the vagaries of love
                the passenger tries to inch next to me,
thunder strikes
                          the bus lurches
rain cloud splits
                       spills, saving me
torn cheap leather seat,
          coconut shell, faded yellow sponge soaks.

spasmodic petri dish
                  decrepit college station terminal
teeming second, what is worse
              closing at 6pm, my ride is late —
a weekend with a control freak boyfriend?
            the skies open up, evil lurks in wait.
or masquerading with a stranger?
           my friend pulls up in the red mustang —
both want to get into my pants.

when the smartphone was non-existent
                  we texted hasty messages
chipped fragments of our existence.

ii.

a god will save me when my own earthy
breasts, those sinless mounds of clay

stare back at me through a selfie,
anchor locket moored to my chest.

a prayer will soothe the scars
your words brand into me.

my words, a slurred confused mixture,
swept away like bent staples.

an insult cloaked in humor will put me
in my place. i touch my naked body

that loves to fuck, my mouth that swears,
my hungry sweat, your molten lust.

iii.

drunk on confidence, spiced rum
and you. limbs, sinewy creepers
of the amazon. veins, pulsate

the radial notches of wrist, say —
o water lily nymph, float,
glide on the dance floor

under the boulevard of stars. body
come undone into knots of
spaghetti straps, stiletto heels.

legs cut into afterglow of sweat,
bare back, eyes, midnight.

you burn with the ambrosia of a lost
youth, fervor of a steed. i burn with

the fever of a middle age,
waiting to play catch-up.

iv.

you finger my clavicle, unbutton
my shirt, touch spaces between

my breasts, tender and wild, fire
and thirst. in the bewitched hour

between pleasure and sleep,
your limbs entangled

with mine, my mouth tastes
earth, sky, the abyss of the oceans

in your eyes. we reach out to meshed
clouds of hair, your tongue sucking

nectar from my skin. how did i
not know your graphical coordinates (x, y).

i have slept with you all afternoon
without an inch of air to part our bodies.

i peel myself from you, your cells alive in me.
did your shoes find many floors, your body

imprint on different sheets before finding me?

v.

blue room, i melt
into its pale walls

lattice of seaweed, kelp

my throat, sandpapered
in a noose of your confessions

the love child you nearly
fathered — a term so feeble

it needs to be curated.
the baby, its veins, an aqua blue

breathing its inheritance —
a bag of sin and regret

i see a canopy of california
poppies, bogs of asphodel, my hair

rooting in the cobalt abyss —
outside russet leaves fall, roar

under dams of logjam, i stare,
unwound beneath this churning guilt.

the season of flaws and accepting —

vi.

on the summer solstice, blue-green hydrangea,
my mailbox full of letters to you you'll never read,

clumps of cumulus disperse into nets of fog.
my instagram account has photos

of me garishly made up in my middle age.
goldenrod and milkweed exude their toxic sap.

amethyst azalea, corona borealis in the heavens.
cast gossamer sheets. chromium sundown slices

angles of your face into curved, chiseled rock.
i asked once if you would chop up destiny

serve it in the sauce of our souls.
i soak in a windex-wiped clarity, carafe

of lemonade with lemon zest lazily orbiting the bottom.
i heard gramophone records are making a comeback.

choked with heat. outside someone has planted
rows of tulip bulbs. gladioli petals find themselves

heard. perhaps that is where we will end up.
crushed, desiccated within the pages of my book.

vii.

this body, a threesome, demerara sugar receptacle,
symmetry rose, tympani of wind chimes, a season

without regret. some nights it is a courtesan on the prowl,
slave to its skin, touching, eyeing, beckoning strange men.

hushed blue ringed moon, a masked chevalier,
watches in frigid desperation. this body, shares in its harvest
— pluck of ({dripping lips}, hanging orbs of breasts).
placid

convexity of back. what lips it may have kissed,
what centers stilled by shuddering fluctuations

of other bodies fucking with their (signature moves).
the windswept night is a raging pack of wolves.

morning is just a key fob away. a hot shower,
housekeeping turns the bedcovers down, it's done.

viii.

mirror, window, errant piece of glass,
watch me bleed.

did i purposefully let you escape
from my sweeping broom?

watch me tangled. unwind me.

i've come
apart, in his skilled
long fingers, in his hands.

sautéed, slathered in butter,
reduced in vino veritas.

taste me. savor me.

my skin burns. he is arjuna
my conqueror, just for a night.

my husband knows.
you've unlaced me, him, us.

an hourglass rewinds — the wine glass
breaks, there's red wine

on the wall, a thousand shards
on the floor.

one lodged in my foot.

you're here. you don't want to be. a midpoint
between him and me, slaking your thirst.

i swallow this — sweet mix of seduction, iron-tinged
blood, adultery.

feet, little pilgrims, carry me, exorcise me.

sedona

red, red sandstone, soft, sedimentary
rock, i hold in my porous palm and

i crumble to felspar, quartz, into,
the concealed crevices of my skin —

a cliff of bones. this textured aquifer
i am, its lithic liesegang band, percolating

liquid flowing into a powdered body of sand.
once i emerged from this earth, writhing,

warped, water in my hollow words. not
for me lush lava, landslide spilling

into the valley. woman, vama, stree, i curve
to the river. i am the bridge on that river,

i am the tilted truss supporting the bridge,
its unwieldy body. i am the planet, i am

the seed planted in my womb. this is blood
that won't wash away, that threads the timelines

of your being. that plunders, pillages lands
that are my own bread basket, my goblet of wine.

i am these that nourish you, nurture you,
i am the nameless nomad whose map you

follow, for there is no beginning, no end.
we must return to the place where the red rocks rise.

spawn

1 —

she scrapes the snow off the car. flashback.
because the root is the soul, because the branch
is never far away from the bud.
pain is a crevasse. open. charred.
some wounds never heal.
she bleeds through them,
nine lives for a cat.
"what do you know about hurt? don't make
up stuff!" she tells this to the wide-eyed
20-year-old with the semi-charmed life
and matching accessories. "you with the moleskine
notebooks, try writing on the dirty floor with a burnt
tongue. make your mark then. let the salt crust
in your eyes. maybe then, you will be ready."

2 —

her palms are a begging bowl,
cupped, chapped. she wanders through the airport,
the gate. random feet. she waits for the hug, the kiss
she never gets. The 'oh my princess, thank you
for the lovely 3 weeks.' it never comes.
he hurls his contempt in her face.

yes, the pain of fathering an under-achieving
daughter. her weight, her sexuality, her poor
choices. "why couldn't you get hired by
microsoft or oracle, some company that
everyone knows about?" tradition. success. society.
these must be splashed in the papers much before
love. she crashes, splinters, an agony of shards,
piled up in guilt. it takes her five solitary months
to build this makeshift castle. he breaks it down
in five minutes or less. the parking meter is running
out of quarters. she drags herself on wobbly legs, holding,
holding to grasp onto anything —
a rudder, an oar, a selfish smile.

3 —

her so called friends. they're all getting married. jubilation
is a miasma. they're calling their folks over for long happy
singsong road trips. they all go away. eventually. fading into
a thousand unsaid betrayals.
she tries them for treason for crimes
they've never committed. one takes the bathmats away,
one her hairbrush,
one kicks her in the solar plexus, so hard.
she doesn't know how to
explain her bloodshot eyes, broken teeth,
cut lips to her boss

the next morning. diversity is a good strategy.
she is hired, the lone

woman in a sea of nerds,
brilliance dripping out of their fingers

into code on a screen. they're all like him. using her.
abandoning her.

she fits right in. she imagines him shaking his head. offspring.

what disappointment.

4 —

cold, bloodless tundra, this. she blooms through the cracks,

an edelweiss in snow. they trample her each time.
stunt her growth.

pale mouth she opens to speak, wood chips fall out.
a dry well, she

waters those around her. they forget her phone number,
her face,

her existence. she is a lost cause, a tough cookie.
they have actual

lives to lead. that don't involve tv dinners
and romance novels

on weekends. she drives by the rehab center,
slowly, purposefully,

hoping someone, anyone in a white coat
will take her hand, lead her

to the wall of all-knowing mirrors and tell her.

"you're beautiful,

you matter, you belong."

land's end

clouds,
those transgressors of dreams,
count time backwards to when i could never tell

skies tumble,
black birds arrange in triangles on sea drenched rocks,
flecks of foam dance on windswept waves.

at the precipice of many a shipwreck, insipid buoyancy,
we once walked, breathing in the same briny air, watching
the cotton candy twilight swirling, hand in hand.

we hike along dreamscapes of unknown trails,
muddy paths perforated
with puddles, our eyes taking in the fresh ferns,
banana slugs, yew berries.

heavy weather brews amidst warping wood,
quiet forests that hide secrets, revealed only to those broken
by someone else.

i used to walk alone. one day i shall walk alone,
in vistas of moonlit ground,
with swaying trees, rains piercing my uncertain veneer
into shreds
that you left me with, again and again,

when i suffocate from your absence, california calling,
i stare at the golden gate bridge, rust-tinged,
trussed across the bay.

i imagine it stacking like a pack of dominoes,
with a lucky penny
in my pocket, the irony, the mockery.

i am grateful, weak, lost, all at once, wondering
how strangers sometimes imprint
their branded names on hearts
that simply won't leave the scene.

9-10/6, south street

i'm 8. my sister is 5. they ship us off to the village every
summer to my grandmother's. blue pillar in the center of
the room. my sister and i walk around it, our only rule:
we should not be able to see each other.

my grandmother, alone, living a quiet life,
keeping the past alive in brass pots.

wooden cradle — creaky, solid, abandoned.

someday, with a son of my own, an only child,
will i be able to let go?

the person who raised a fine man, now obsolete.

widowhood — deserted island that eats itself
alive with acid.

my grandmother, hides her tenderness, delivers babies,
carries heavy water-pots.

a chorus of temple bells coupled with heavy chanting
fills the street.

the smell of sacred ash floats out like dust. people stop in
their tracks, close their eyes, murmur their prayers.

four generations at shanghumukham beach, kerala

cowrie
beach shell, brittle
caught in a tidal swell
flung onto thorium–striated
black sand, empty.

arabian sea, conch-bearer
of mollusks —
what rises in your crest,
what sinks in your trough?

orange rose blush is this sunset,
a syrup of muscovado.

my family — four generations, the youngest
in the water's spritz, the oldest
far off on a concrete bench.

the rest scattered in the sand,
each one a step closer to the fizz
of sea salt, a step further
from the grand finale.

bow bridge, central park, nyc

cast-iron ripples

                        molten steel-cut lake.

i stroll toward the archer's hand

                    that wields a violinist's bow

from the ramble to cherry hill.

urns, rise from abutments.

                    i adorn in my hair the reluctant

lilies from the conservatory.

you're here, my beloved husband,

                    i find you here in metallic winters,

in beauty's summers.

is that you on the balustrade,

                    in its intricate etchings?

i wait and watch — an arrow, a glance,

                  how they stage a coup, seize the perimeter,

unseat my unwilling heart.

the dancing girl of mohenjo-daro

it's my day out at the art museum.
the freer and sackler galleries.
the bronze statue of the dancing girl mocks me.
one hand

on her hip,
she challenges me to guess her name.
real girl in the indus valley
civilization sits on a parapet,

red sandstone on her skin, watches
the tulsi plant in the center
of the courtyard. raindrops drench her,
ricochet off the bricks.

jasmine petals flutter from her hair
onto her tanned fingers.
bangles size up her arms,
urgency clasps them to jangling wrists.

clouds wring last drops of monsoon,
sponge it clean. water
mixes with the muddy gully,
carves ravines on her wet palms.

she's filled with dread. that time again, a hall of strangers.

for silver anklets to pound uneven sandy floors. for the sun
to sink into the indus. she must talk often to herself,
in the paddy

fields, scrawl her name in the mud. she must hang her hopes
on mango branches, dream of escape.
she must braid her hair

with fireflies, that hiss in the crypt of her heart.
yet she stands,
feminine, sacred — here, now.
i examine my own wrists, my feet

encased in casual converse sneakers. is she a goddess?
a slave? whom does she love? does she live, like me, for love?

sonagachi

her words — whatever erodes me/deposits this sediment,
this mixed identity,
           i stand before you, a jasmine in a field of violets.

there is her body — citadel, guards her cavernous
womb — someone
forgets to shut the door. swirl, the wind's whiplash rushes in.

night is a fortress, its jaded ramparts fail
to keep intruders out.
this castle, built with a portcullis to a drawbridge,
leads to her ruin.

another like her, waits, in the moat of her amniotic fluid.
a woman-child, her trapped identity belonging
to her vagina's highest bidder.

her birth in the flesh market,
in a makeshift room of stained sheets,
lust-cloaked air thick with mosquitoes and moisture,
brings no joy.

no game of coquette here, no foreplay, only tears long dried,
buried under garish makeup, so many bills to pay.

she throws away the condom, refuses HIV testing,
outranks the others' sales.

another day, another batch of underage girls,
trafficked into bonds of slavery.

she envies their nubility, wonders which one is from her
native place, fingers a cheap ring, the only link to her
mother's betrayal.

no dna test, no father figure,
nothing to promise, nothing to forgive,
she wraps herself around her knees,
conjures warrior names for the unborn,
durga, arjun.

her thoughts — born to sin, guilty without trial, burned
meteors under half the crimson sky.

exodus

mother!

let me cut paper fragments,
                    craft your origami dreams

trace chapped fingers in sandy dunes —
                    faces of now nameless friends

skip stones along elusive maps,
                    my feet, barren & scaly, cross borders

play hopscotch, my tiles break
                    too easily, you rest under charred trees

i make you finger puppets, you watch
                    them talk, of a home left behind, a home

that exists still, morphed by shells & mortar.
                    now it is night, you point to galaxies

in the sky, i've heard there could be life
                    on enceladus now. is that where we're

going? i was your shadow, your
                    safe haven. we run to each other now,

rush into our arms. i don't know what home is,
                    but i know this. we have it in each other.

this is how we save lives. in fractured sanctuaries.
          in disjoint geographies. a small part of history, lives.

bar island, maine

i cross bridge street & walk along the edge
of bar harbor. my feet gauge the high tide,

my silver toe ring latches onto an unfamiliar
gastropod. i scoop up the pebbles, gravel,

watch sand slip through my wrinkled
fingers. the afternoon is tired, late, sun

is a weak light under a cloud blanket,
rampant marine life is bathed in sheen.

low tide sets, i watch crabs scuttle to safety.
mussels, clamshells — barnacled beyond

recognition, scattered treasure. my sandals
crunch them further into calcified oblivion.

i see the waters recede — the aquatic curtains
are drawn, stage is set for the big crossing.

ninety minutes of isolation till the tide sets in again.

details *(widowed mother/only son)*

1 —

all over his village, the houses, not yet alive

        not yet dying — blemished alabaster walls peel,

stories to tell, words to recount.

        on the outskirts, paddy fields spread —

a checkered handkerchief.

        he is overcome in a choked profusion

of tamarind pods, banana leaves, palm fronds,

        a stray hibiscus flower.

his house is a tomb of ghosts, a black box

        — wealth is blind — it resonates

with acoustics of betrayal.

        this land, its crops, this gold, its

craftsmanship, these will outlive their breaths,

        outlast the ashes finely dusting them.

2 —

if the hours could speak, how long would they burn,

    be held accountable for this loneliness, this suffering?

their life is a sloshing water pot on her waist,
a complete revolution

    of her rosary beads, one whole minute of the spigot

left open in his granary, grains spilling, dissolved.

    he puts away the handmade wooden toys, hides

in the antechamber, tucked away in his own miniature

    market; she grinds the coconut and green chilies

in the wet grindstone, then makes the dosa batter.

        these images settle in his mind, before
        the property dispute,

five years old, suddenly homeless, suddenly an adult.

3 —

these tales are held in place, with clothespins

       in the backyard — tales of a house, a field,

a tube-well, stacked firewood, shaved locks of hair.

    the old now cannot pinpoint a name, an ownership,

forgotten ages ago, in a decrepit home, now sold.

4 —

sometimes his thoughts will trespass this house,

   intersecting with his mother's, they will find common

ground — once upon a time, there was a bride
and a marriage,

       a baby and laughter and sunlit terraces

and boyhood dreams. now all they have are documents,

    details, a penumbral profusion of darkness, light.

kurinji flowers

blues, stitched across
rust-red valleys
streak the earth,
contain the spring,
will the rain
to be patient.

they carve my eyes,
with the melancholy
of a young girl's heart,
its approaching
tempest.

fair & lovely

pink. the wallpaper.
the dresses. the dolls.
ribbons on braids.
bracelets, earrings, bows.
the perfume, mom's vanity.

teen vogue. cute boys.
diet pills. acne cream.
crushes. photogenic angles.
smile more. frown less.
cross my legs.
can i cut my hair?
no, grow it out.
be sure to shave your legs.

nail polish. pink doesn't
suit me anymore. am i
playing too much in the sun?
don't — you'll get too dark.
i might need a fairness cream.
but i must play indoors and run —
or i'll get too fat. i don't care
if models are airbrushed, i want
to look like that! you, hah!

reality check, you're all brain.
stop looking in the mirror. let's
get a dictionary for an 8-year-old.
understand 'ugly' 'fat' 'ordinary'.
keep your eyes to the ground.

the fat one

fatty. chunky. so many names.
they call out to her in silent sound waves.

no judgments they say.
she believes them.

gullible girl, she tries to fit in. desperation like drops
of excess sweat in her armpits.

la di dah society chatter.
their glances say all she needs to know.

she's overdressed, no spot of skin visible. extra polite.

no judgments they say.
while talking about their marathons and diets.

she believes them.

she puts up a wall of self-defense —
it dissolves simply like biscuits in tea.

how can a person so large be so invisible
how can a person not sleep

because she has no dreams, the voices said.
because she needs a city of resigned acceptance that she
will never ever be

in anyone's dream.

she believes them.

pi day

the wall street journal reports this. it must be true.
pi day. super pi day. once in a lifetime occurrence.

3.1415926 … a child, she once took a compass,
drew a circle. she measured its diameter, calculated its

circumference. it came to 22/7. or ϖ as we affectionately
know it today. that was her first constant. in a world

of strangers, planes, new homes and screaming
families, pi never changed. she simply had to pencil

it into the back of her notebook or pull out a calculator —
it returned her affections the same way. never-changing,

always reassuring. a woman now, she planned her wedding
around it. there had to be apple pie,
bouquets of 3.14 flowers,

a veil embroidered with the greek alphabet pi in it
perhaps? and of course, the ceremony had to take place

at 9.26am march 14th, 2015. that she knew would seal
the deal. she would tell herself that, despite the lies,

lipstick stains on collars. did it not mean that the marriage
would last as long as the digits of pi? it had to! there were

pi t-shirts and pi-neapple cakes and pi tattoos to keep her
grounded. who needs love when there is science,
data and math?

she would tell herself that three years later, alone, friendless,
walking the streets of princeton spotting the albert einstein

lookalikes on his birthday.
maybe this spring the dahlias would
bloom in perfect multiples.
things needed to make sense. then

all would be right in this world, spinning on its axis
every 24 hours.

girls' night out

a ghost of a line, where borders get redefined
by the moment. syria burns, its people flee,

refugees now, without a home. children, women
first. radicals next. the persecution continues.

npr reports it so. the headlines tells me so i can
coolly express my horror, with a cocktail held

in hand. in soirees hosted with glittery women,
fake plastic smiles aplenty, i mingle, stand out

like a lime in a martini. i'm sized up, my car,
clothes, a faint horrified gasp at my unbranded

bag. how on earth can one forget to apply lipstick
when the ebola virus has claimed 730 lives in africa?

we can now move on to other things, our children,
vacations, diamonds, club memberships. why break

the bubble. i'd rather focus on my nail polish than tank
shells. somewhere another mother buries her newborns

in the ground, while around her, god unleashes
his fury — sorry, men claiming to be god's own

emissaries kidnap, capture, behead, all in the name
of — what? love? darn, it is 11p.m. air kissed, i drive home.

two pictures of my sister in my head
After Dorianne Laux

it is a pose like no other, a sepia-toned attempt to capture
what world she inhabits, mirror of a dusty native village,
creeper-sprawled tree, two dolls in her hands. one she
holds with the confidence of belonging, the right of
an owner, the other, unsure, waiting for a playmate, a
sister she has heard of but has never seen or can't recall.
barefoot on the stony soil, restless, a kindergarten frock
slightly crumpled, the hint of a crease across her bushy
brows, hair neatly swept back.

this one is years later, in color. her flesh melted away, her
skin glowing on a bony frame, the body i always would
envy, even two children later. long black hair, washed with
the fragrance of coconut oil on a weekend, caught-in-
headlights eyes. she stands in front of guests, the words not
coming out. when prompted to say hello, she runs
to our sparse bedroom, long-legged behind the cotton
floral curtain.

he is a devout, simple, sincere man. unlike the cad she
fell for, but she does not want either. she moves to
the balcony. i ply her with gifts from america — a cd
player with fancy headphones, a stethoscope. something
with a string attached to me that will prevent her from
contemplating the leap. no one tells her what to do —
under pressure — incensed nerves, bulging blood vessels,
afraid to breathe. on her wedding day, her sari blooms
into a gossamer of pink organza. cynosure of all eyes, her
glance fixates on the fire. her face a dead stone bust, no

fur or antler, she smiles. a tube light on the verge of a fuse. she lowers her eyes, a perfect blushing bride, waiting for the moment the garland hangs around her neck-branch, knowing the deer has already been hunted down.

antelope canyon, page, arizona

we descend
into dune-like depths
hand in hand

the places
where water runs through rocks,
life, that meaningless thrum

of days into months, years,
decades of caption and photograph
breast and thigh

intense and invisible
a crack, a corkscrew,
arches cut into sweat

and sigh
we fit into each other, wordless
without ink, hotel paper

we transfer ourselves
into a medium of similar frequencies
skin and sand erode

in a flash flood
of climax, striated rays
of hide-n-seek sunlight fall

upon us, in a dance, the way
we explore our bodies at night

a sonic boom in the earth's bed
warm, satisfied, knowing
with no rush

to be remembered,
no condition to belong
it's not too narrow to imagine

cinnabar and carmine,
sunbeam and rainwater,
the rivers rushing through

washing away sins of sandstone —
royal purple, sunburnt orange
mixed with our own gasps of awe

blood moon, suicide point, kodaikanal

i am 10 again, 1984. there is a tour guide
who smells of cigarette smoke. nauseating.

no gps or maps or sightseeing brochures.
the grass is cloaked in dew. proudly he tells us

of the main attraction. lovers take their lives here.
lonely hearts. sad repressed souls. my innocence,

trapped, struggles to escape. a butterfly in a bell jar.
i don't understand. i want to know why anyone would

do such a thing. he says this is a special night. points
towards the sky. it is churning powdered red chilies

in a blender. like holi in the heavens. the moon is cloaked
in crimson. bloodshot. it's the night of the eclipse. people

are in their homes. why are we here? is it an omen —
will roots twist around my ankles? the riven cliffs beckon.

it is a steep drop to an inky abyss.
is it better to jump, i ask him.
he looks at me strangely.
i ask this question to another man

thirty years later. it is 2014. i am 40.
he squeezes my hand.
showers me with poetry.
kisses the words i write with my fingers.

he loves that i am dusky.
he loves my eyes. my lips. my legs.
he wishes he had married me. made love to me.
had my children.

i am drawn into his thought-spiral.
will i return to that night
that won't end?
the night we talked and talked and didn't sleep.

or the night he left me?
i want to run towards those cliffs again.
it is a jigsaw puzzle.
i feel the jumbled pieces coming together

in my eclipsed heart as i run. the wind chafes my cheeks,
combs my hair. the cosmos enters me. it's a free-fall.

Acknowledgement

Deeply grateful to my Drew community of faculty and friends, without whom this book may have never been created. And to the various journals and anthologies where my work has found a home.

The Olentangy Review, "lip gloss"

(b)OINK zine, "how to break a married woman"

DIN magazine — NMSU, "eight days till the new moon"

The Wild Word magazine, "details (widowed mother/only son)"

Tin Lunchbox review, "four generations at shanghumukham beach, kerala", & "northeast well, kerala"

Jaggery Lit, "kurinji flowers"

The Electronic Pamphlet, "fair and lovely"

Sonic Boom, "august"

Colors of refuge, "exodus"

To my family and friends for your loyal undying support, to the Writers' Circle for nurturing a fledgling talent and to my poets' groups for keeping my pen alive.

Thank you.

www.ingramcontent.com/pod-product-compliance
Lightning Source LLC
Chambersburg PA
CBHW030513130626
46549CB00007B/2981